Creating Calm From Chaos

Help for the Frazzled Parent of a Strong-Willed Child

THERESA LUMOS, MA, NCC, LPC

Copyright © 2010 Theresa Lumos
All rights reserved.

ISBN: 1451542151
ISBN-13: 9781451542158
Library of Congress Control Number: 2010903546

*This book is lovingly dedicated to my mother,
who always believes in me.*

ACKNOWLEDGEMENTS

I would like to take this opportunity to acknowledge my husband, Rev. Denny Lumos, who has gained momentum as the book became a reality, and who has demonstrated his belief in me by asking what topic I will choose for my second book. I would like to acknowledge my family members who have helped with editing: my sister Margie Hale, my niece Amy Richardson, and my mother Joyce White. I would like to acknowledge two of my sisters, Pattie Brooks and Debbie Hohimer, who helped me with the title for the book. Debbie, not only came up with the final choice for the title, but she was also an encourager and consultant in the development of the Effective Time-Out method. Furthermore, I would like to thank the rest of my family for their support of this endeavor: my father Rev. Harry White, Vickie Warren (and her children), and Rich White, (and his girls).

I would be remiss if I did not acknowledge the families with whom I work, who offer a constant path to learning by looking to me for answers. I am grateful to Mandy Erwin-Smith for her work in helping to gather the testimonials.

Lastly, I want to acknowledge my children, James and Bethany, the two who were strong-willed and challenged me at every turn, and Caleb, who was compliant yet who taught me the most about surrendering to ultimate authority.

Most importantly, I want to acknowledge my God, who has administered the lessons, even the hardest ones, and then held my hand.

Table of Contents

Chapter 1: An Introduction to the Strong-Willed Child 1

Chapter 2: Who Needs This Book? 7

Chapter 3: Effective Time Outs 15

    The Effective Time-Out (ETO) 17

    What You Do When Your Child is in Time-Out 23

    How Important is it for my Child to Put his Hands on his

    Knees?. 26

    What Happens if my Child Hits Me or Calls Me Names?. 28

Chapter 4: The Safety Hold. 31

    What can I Expect in Doing the Safety Hold? 38

Chapter 5: The Surrender (The Child's, Not Yours) 45

Chapter 6: What About my Child's Spirit?. 31

Chapter 7: What to do in Public Places 53

    What to do when Shopping 53

    At a Restaurant 55

    At a Relative's or a Friend's House 56

    In the Car. 56

    In Church or Other Like Settings 58

Chapter 8: Monster Time-Outs and Total Time-Outs. 59

    Monster Time-Outs 59

    Total Time-Outs. 60

Chapter 9: What do I do with my Other Children 63

    What Do I Do with My Baby?. 63

    What About my Younger Children who are not Infants? 65

    What About my Older Children? 66

Chapter 10: What About Day Care/Sitters?. 67

Chapter 11: Bedtime 69

    The First Step 69

    The Second Step 70

    The Third Step. 72

    The Fourth Step. 72

    A Typical Bedtime Scenario from the Beginning 73

Chapter 12: What Children Should Not Have This Form of Discipline . 79

Chapter 13: Testimonials. 81

CHAPTER ONE:
AN INTRODUCTION
TO THE STRONG-WILLED CHILD

After I became a parent for the first time, my mother commented that my new baby was "demanding." I didn't understand. My baby was just being a baby, I thought. Babies are demanding. The little guy knew what he wanted, and since he could not talk, he had to "pitch a fit" until I figured out what he was trying to communicate to me. What else could he do?

I did not realize what my mother meant about my firstborn being a demanding baby until my second son was born 21 months later. This second-born was a compliant child, smiling easily and being patient. He seemed content to just go with the flow, laughing and cooing wherever he was planted.

As these two boys grew, my firstborn continued to be a challenge at times. There were days I just stood looking at him, helplessly wondering what a good parent should do about his latest caper. I somehow muddled through, always second-guessing myself and forever receiving unsolicited advice from well-meaning friends, relatives, church nursery workers, people in the grocery store, etc. Usually the advice was that he needed a good spanking.

When these boys were ten and twelve years of age, we were blessed with another baby, albeit a girl, this time. I soon discovered that she had a strong will that could rival her elder brother's. Because I had been through it once before, I may have done a little better the second time around, but oftentimes, I was plagued with doubts and fears that I was not doing the right things for her.

When my youngest started kindergarten, I began teaching in the public school system. My experience as the mother of two strong-willed children served me well in the classroom as I dealt with the challenges brought on by having at least four strong-willed students in my classroom each year. I researched strategies and honed my skills, learning from each of these interesting children a little more about what worked to motivate them and to garner cooperation.

While teaching school, I also began work on my master's degree in community counseling. I knew I had developed a knack for working with difficult children, and I wanted to help these children and their parents. Upon graduating with my master's degree and earning my license in professional counseling, I went to work for a child therapy center.

As a children's therapist, I was expected to be the expert, and was often called upon to help parents with out-of-control pre-school children. Again, I researched and learned from the parents and children. I used experiences of my own, as well as experiences of co-workers who had worked with difficult children. I prayed for guidance, and I used an "instinct" about what it was these strong-willed children ultimately needed. I discovered a formula that I have honed and expanded until it worked amazing wonders on strong-willed children between the ages of two and six. I offer it to all harried parents who are searching for help in raising a difficult child.

If you use this strategy, following the procedures to a "T," you can once again enjoy parenthood instead of feeling exhausted and inept. However, this method takes commitment in two areas: you must be consistent and you must be persistent. I have come across a couple of parents who just didn't want to make their child unhappy, even temporarily, in order to have a happier child a week later, as well as for the rest of the child's life. Yes, the child is unhappy about having his or her power taken by the parent, but the parent who uses this method inevitably reports to me that in the long run, the child is happier, more compliant, and more child-like instead of being like a three-foot-tall Hitler, acting as dictator of the family.

The parents of strong-willed preschoolers who come to our center often wonder why their children are so defiant and difficult. The answer probably lies in genetics. A child inherits his or her strong will. However, when a strong-willed child is put into a lenient environment, it creates a monster, so to speak. Parents who had their compliant child or children first, and then are blessed with a strong-willed child, are the ones who struggle the most. They have tasted success in parenting. Why, they wonder, are their strategies not working this time with this child?

On the other hand, parents who birth their strong-willed child first, must put up with their friends who have compliant children. These friends may look down on their struggling friend and make him or her feel like a complete failure as a parent. They do not understand that strong-willed children have special needs. One of the most important needs is a firm, structured environment with hard and fast rules. We will get to the specifics of that later.

When strong-willed mothers come to our center with a strong-willed child, I know we have a very good chance for success. However, if the child inherited his strong will from the father and the mother is now single and trying to raise the child on her own, her task will seem more difficult. The important truth to remember is that it can be done. She just has to work harder at persistence—not giving up.

"Hanging in there" is difficult for the mom who does not have a will that equals the magnitude of her child's will. She must summon her courage and persistence from deep inside and use it often and fully. She must give it her best without

4 | CREATING CALM FROM CHAOS

the support of a partner to cheer her on and to take on some of the responsibility in helping to discipline her child.

Persistency is important, but so is consistency. Inconsistency is the downfall of most parents. We let things slide one day and discipline for it the next. Something gets a time-out one day, and the next day a verbal reprimand is all that is given. Consistency, no matter how tired the parent, no matter where the parent happens to be, no matter the circumstances for the child that day, no matter what—that is the key.

Another common pitfall is for mothers who have a difficult child to make excuses for him or her. The child is tired, bored, just returning from a visit with dad, etc. I ask you, is it okay to be mean and ugly if one is tired? No. It is important for the parent to teach that even when one is tired, one still needs to be polite and kind. That is the message our children need to learn. Otherwise, your child will think it is okay to be disrespectful, and then blame it on being tired. You are going to be a severely beat-up parent when the child becomes a teenager. You don't want to give him the ammunition now to shoot you later.

If you find that you yourself are cranky when you are tired, stop it. Be a good example. It is okay to say that you are tired, but model respect to others in spite of feeling tired, and then go to bed early. That is being a good example. If you are a single parent, once the children go to bed, you go to bed early that night. If you say to me, "But my children stay up until I go to bed," that needs to stop. I have a chapter in this book on "Bedtime." Once you employ those methods, you will be getting your children to bed an hour or two before you go to bed. That hour or two will be your time. If you have a strong-willed child, you need to have a little time to yourself every day. Do the work necessary now so that you can have rest and peace on a regular basis just a little further down the road. The work you do now will certainly pay off then.

As a single parent, you need some time alone in the evening to talk on the phone without interruptions, to check your

AN INTRODUCTION TO THE STRONG-WILLED CHILD | 5

email, to prepare for the next day, etc. If you are a couple, you need some couple time without the children around to interrupt. Couples of strong-willed children often report to me that bedtime is an exhausting and frustrating routine that leaves them less than in the mood for intimacy. Often, strong-willed children sleep with the parent or parents. Why? Because the child insists. That needs to change because it is not best for the family as a whole. Dealing with the strong-willed child means changing areas that used to cater only to the strong-willed child. After making these changes, you will see how the family as a whole is now functioning better.

"Consistency" and "persistency"—write down these two words and plaster them all over your house at the beginning of this new journey. Most likely, you are going to have a rough first week, as will your child. But the second week is better for both of you, and the third is even better than the second. The entire rest of your life will be easier. Trust me. I see it happening every day!

CHAPTER TWO:
WHO NEEDS THIS BOOK?

Well, probably you do. If you have picked up this book, you are probably searching for something that will help you raise your strong-willed child without pulling out all of your hair. This is the book.

Let me begin by briefly telling you who doesn't need this book. If you have a child who wilts when you give him a correcting look across a crowded room, you don't need this book. If you have a child who sits repentantly in time-out, then apologizes to you and begs your forgiveness, before leaving the time-out chair, determined to sin no more, you don't need this book. If you have a child for whom people beg to baby-sit, you don't need this book.

However, you need this book if any of these situations fit you and your child:

1. Your child refuses to look at you across a crowded room, because she knows she is doing something wrong, and she doesn't want to be stopped.

2. Your child refuses time-outs or any punishment. When you have resorted to spankings, he says, "That didn't hurt."

3. Your child finally completes her minutes of time-out, giving you dirty looks the entire time, then leaves the time-out chair and immediately misbehaves again.

4. Your child has been kicked out of daycare, friends don't want to socialize with you if you are going to bring "him," and even Grandma cringes when you come to her door with your child in tow.

5. Your child can throw a temper tantrum at the drop of a hat, and will continue to do so, not even noticing that you are sitting in a corner, having a nervous breakdown.

If you have a child who demands the lion's share of your time and attention, if you have a child that everyone in the family works to keep "happy," it is time to take back control of your life. Just as you would not give the steering wheel to your 3-year-old to let him chauffeur the family around town, you cannot give control of the family to your child. You are the reigning royalty, the king and/or queen of your house, and you must take back your rightful place on the throne else your kingdom shall perish.

I have several purposes for writing this book. One of my intentions is to empower you as the parent. Remember that you are much more powerful than you even realize. Your authority will be recognized if you become more demanding. If you don't want to be "mean" to your kids, if you want to be more of a "friend" to your kids, if you want them to obey you because they love you and want to please you, you are going to have to wake up and smell the coffee.

WHO NEEDS THIS BOOK? | 9

If you have a strong-willed child, you were not blessed with the kind of child who does well in a lenient environment. You have been blessed with a strong-willed child instead. "Blessed?" you might ask. Yes, blessed. Your strong-willed child will give you less worry later. When he is trudging along through the most difficult trials in his life, and does not even stumble, you will see how that strong-will is serving him well. You will see how his persistence is what is keeping him sane, focused, and determined. But for now, your strong-willed child needs you to provide a strong foundation. Upon the foundation that you supply, he will build a structure that you both will admire in his adulthood.

Many experts in the field of child development agree that strong-willed children are born that way. They are demanding from the beginning. Parents, like me, who have strong-willed children and also have compliant children, will tell you that the two children were different from the start. If you provide your strong-willed child with structure (his foundation), you are giving your child the best gift you could possibly give.

There is a place for strong-willed people in the world. They can accomplish much. We need them. But they have to learn to self-discipline or they may go down the wrong path instead. Many people in prison were strong-willed children, (also known as "hard-headed"), but they did not have the structure to teach them self-discipline, sometimes called self-control. When you teach a strong-willed child how to have self-control, you are creating a leader—a hero.

People wonder why Attention Deficit Hyperactivity Disorder (ADHD) and Oppositional Defiant Disorder (ODD) seem more prevalent now than 50 years ago. I have a theory about that. Fifty years ago homes and schools were much more structured. Moms were more likely to be at home, keeping things running smoothly. Teachers demanded their students be quieter in the classroom than what is expected today. In fact, today it is a compliment to have a noisy class—"Oh, there's always something going on in there!" If the classroom is quiet, that just seems too old-fashioned and boring.

10 | CREATING CALM FROM CHAOS

Some people think that children in a quiet classroom are not learning as much as in the noisy classrooms. The truth is that ADHD children are usually overwhelmed in a noisy, busy classroom. Furthermore, these classrooms often do not teach the self-control that is absolutely necessary for the ADHD and the ODD children.

Children *need* structure and discipline. They thrive in those environments that demand it. Back in my day (the good old days), children walked down the hallways quietly. Two classes could meet in the hallway, pass each other, and still maintain absolute silence. Now I see elementary children walking down the hallway chattering away as they are in a "line," (certainly not single-file), on the way to music or back from recess. Children are no longer *required* to have the self-control that was expected in previous generations. Having self-control is very important in the lifetime success of people.

More and more research is being conducted which validates time and time again that we, as parents and teachers, have concentrated too much on a child's self-esteem and too little on his self-control. Teaching the important concept of self-control has been neglected, and now we are paying the price. We have egotistical children with inflated self-esteem and little self-control. We are creating children who bully the adults in their lives.

So now let's turn our attention to your strong-willed child. How do I know that your child is strong-willed? You're looking for some help, aren't you? Now that you have tried a number of things, why don't you try the method I am promoting in this book? To the max. All the way. Totally do it. I guarantee that you won't be sorry. Let me give you a few examples of the children I have counseled.

Stevie* was an out-of-control three-year-old who presented at my office with his biological parents and his one-year-old brother. Mom had taken Stevie to the doctor, and brought in a prescription slip with Stevie's diagnosis—Attention Deficit/Hyperactivity Disorder. While I gathered information for the assessment and worked at establishing a therapeutic relationship with the parents, Stevie stomped on the toys I had brought to the family therapy room for him to play with. He was loud and disrespectful to everyone.

At one point his father tried to pick him up to talk to him, and Stevie went into a tantrum. Dad set him back down and shrugged his shoulders in helpless confusion about what to do. When Mom tried to put Stevie into time-out, he began hitting, kicking, and biting her. The parents explained how this little boy had turned their lives upside-down. They no longer got invitations to their friends' homes. Grandparents refused to baby-sit. They had to stop going to church because Stevie was so disruptive, and they never went to a restaurant anymore. They feared for the safety of their younger child.

After using my methods for two weeks, they came for their third therapy session. Stevie was quiet and self-controlled. He entered the room. He stood quietly for a while, and then picked up a children's book I had laid on a table, and took it to his father. He whispered, "Would you read this to me?" His father pulled Stevie onto his lap, and they quietly enjoyed a book while mom and I talked about the changes in Stevie and what it had meant to her family.

Mom said that everywhere they went, people asked, "What happened to Stevie?" He was getting much positive attention. They went to visit grandparents, and the grandparents were so pleased by the change in Stevie that they suggested a camping trip for everyone. This had been out of the question two weeks earlier. She had tears in her eyes as she reported to me, "And you know what? *He* is happier." What a positive change in the lives of this family!

Andrew* was another child who came to the therapy center. Andrew was being raised by his grandparents. Kindergarten was going to start in a little over a month, and Andrew was still acting far too impulsively and immaturely to be a successful kindergartener. Grandma was concerned that he was going to be a behavior problem in school.

At the end of our first session, in which Grandma took back her rightful place as queen, Andrew went over to a pad of paper he had been doodling on earlier in the session. He sat down and wrote his name in a line. His grandmother was amazed. She looked at me and asked, "Do you see that? We have been trying to teach Andrew how to write his name so he will be ready for kindergarten, but he would always write the letters all over the page instead of putting them together in a line. Look at that. This is the first time that Andrew has written his name in a line."

What a metaphor for what had just taken place in Andrew's brain! He had just gotten his thinking straightened out. He came to realize he had to conform to the requirements of his grandmother. Yes, we need free thinkers. But the child must learn when to be a leader and when to be a follower. He must be able to follow authority figures all of his life.

Everyone has authority figures to which they must answer, even adults: our boss, the police, and our "higher power." We must be able to submit to authority. There is nothing scarier to a five-year-old, than to realize that he is in charge. Andrew probably felt relieved when Grandma took over as the authority figure, and it was no longer up to him.

What if you were suddenly put in charge of our nation's government, thrown into the position of President of the United States? Cool, you might think at first, until you had to actually use that authority to make an important decision that would determine the fate of our nation. Then suddenly, you may panic and wish you were back to being a regular citizen. This is the panic experienced by children who are given too much authority within the family. It is frightening, and it makes them angry. Someone should be taking care of me, they think; I don't need all this pressure! But they try to exercise that authority as best they can. They just do not know what to do with all the power that has been afforded them. They begin to abuse their power.

Now let's look at Trevor*. Trevor was one of the first children I saw. He taught me much about working with the strong-willed child. His mother was a single mom trying to do the best she could. Trevor was an out-of-control three-

WHO NEEDS THIS BOOK? | 13

year-old. He was getting up in the mornings and getting into the refrigerator. He broke eggs, poured out milk, and made a huge mess before Mom was even out-of-bed.

When Mom gave Trevor his first Effective Time-Out in my office, Trevor wouldn't stay in the chair. His mother placed him back into the chair 110 times before he stayed for the first time. He still holds the record. Your child may be even more determined. (Write and tell me if you put your child back in the chair more than 110 times in one episode). I told his mother that all she had to do was to put Trevor back into the chair one more time than the number of times that Trevor got out of the chair, and she would win. "And when mama wins, you both win; and when the child wins, you both lose," I told her. I encouraged her to keep it up, and she did. After 110 times, he decided, "Hey, this isn't working. I guess I am going to have to just sit here." And he did.

Strong-willed children are necessary in our world. They grow up to be strong-willed adults. When a strong-willed person manages to gain self-control to rule over his strong-will, he has just born a winning combination. That is the kind of determination of which heroes are made. Life is tough. Those who can come through hardships with their spirit and their laugh intact are the strong-willed ones. They are the survivors. They are the thrivers.

*Names have been changed

CHAPTER THREE:
EFFECTIVE TIME OUTS

I know what you're thinking. I have tried EVERYTHING. Nothing works. Time-outs don't work for my child. I put him in time-out, and he gets out. I put him in again, and he gets out again. He gets irritated with me. As I work to get him back in the chair, he screams and struggles. He won't go. He lets me know that I can't make him. He sometimes even hits or kicks me. He screams in protest.

This is the common response for a strong-willed child. They are not easy to guide. In desperation, you either give up completely (Message to child: "You win. You can do as you please, and I can't stop you"), or you spank him. If you spank him, you feel better in knowing that he needed discipline and you delivered it, but he is walking away after just 5 seconds of discipline with a look of triumph on his face. He may even mutter, "That didn't hurt." So you may spank him again—hard, and he says through teary eyes, "That still didn't hurt." Defiance is spilling out of your child. Now what?

Never fear. Help is here. Let's start by understanding the dual purpose of doing the time-out, and then I will teach you a unique and special way of doing time-outs to accomplish

16 | CREATING CALM FROM CHAOS

that purpose. I call them Effective Time-Outs. By first understanding the two-fold purpose, you will have a foundation upon which to stand as questions or problems crop up. Soon, it all will come naturally to you since it all makes sense.

Let me start with a confession. Two years ago, I was given—actually I earned (a very important differentiation)—a speeding ticket. I was a few blocks from my home going 42 in a 30 mile-an-hour zone. Now, imagine if you will, that the officer angrily walked up to my car and began yelling at me for speeding. Then, let's say he spent 20 minutes carefully explaining the many good reasons that I should slow down. Finally, he ended our encounter by begging me to "Please, stop speeding."

I probably would have found this amusing. However, it may not have slowed me down. Let's say I keep speeding everyday going to work, and he stops me most of the time. Sometimes, he just lets me go. But when he does stop me, he only yells at me, or tries to reason with me, or begs me to not speed. On mornings when he does not stop me, I will feel that I have won, that I have beat him at his game. Pretty soon, he is just going to be one big annoyance in my morning routine. This officer of the law would not have one iota of my respect.

However, the preceding scenario is not what happened to me. In actuality, the officer pulled me over, and he treated me politely. There was no anger, no lecture, and no attempt to try to reason with me. He just got right to business. After he handed me a ticket with an $85.00 fine, he told me to go on my way and to drive safely, and that is what I did. (I didn't speed again for about a month). That is what we need to do when we discipline our children. Be matter-of-fact. Be respectful. Make a predictable consequence. We need to give them a ticket! And the consequence must be big enough that the misbehavior is not worth doing again. At least, not anytime soon.

Spankings do not work when administered as the usual course of discipline for a strong-willed child. A strong-willed child can come out of a spanking just as defiant as he was when he went into a spanking. For that matter, he can sit in the time-out chair giving the parent dirty looks, whining as he asks if time is up yet, then come out of the chair after his three or four minute sentence, and have the same defiance that he had when he went into the chair. He can walk away from the time-out chair with an air of "Why did you interrupt me this way? Can't you see I have things to do?"

The Effective Time-Out (ETO)

What will work and why? Strong-willed children must do their time-outs in a different way. They have to sit with their hands on their knees. Why? Simply because that is what you are requesting. The only way for them to complete their time-out is for them to comply with your request—totally comply. In fact, they must be sitting with their hands on their knees in order for the time-out to even start. *See Illustration on the following page.*

Usually one minute per year of age is the accepted standard for the amount of time-out to be administered. However, when I am coaching parents in doing the first Effective Time-Out with younger children (ages 2 to 4), I have the parents to give the child a 10-second time-out. That means that the parent slowly counts to ten once the child is in the Effective Time-Out position (which is explained later).

The purpose of the ten seconds is to teach the child that time-out has a beginning, has an end, and there is behavior expected in the middle. I usually recommend that the parent continue with the 10-second time-out for about a week. Once the child is successful with the 10-second time-out, we move to 20 seconds. Once the child is successful with 20 seconds (usually in just a couple of days), we move to 30 seconds, and the parent no longer counts out loud. The parent tells the child that he or she (the parent) will observe the child and let the child know when his time-out has started. Before the time can start, the child must be complying with

18 | CREATING CALM FROM CHAOS

the parent in maintaining the Effective Time-Out stance—
(hands on knees, sitting quietly, holding still, and having a
pleasant look on his face).

EFFECTIVE TIME OUTS | 19

The parent also will let the child know if time has to be restarted because the child begins to wiggle or talk. Once the child is complying with the expected time-out stance (hands on knees, sitting up straight) and behavior (quiet and without anger) the parent lets the child know so that time can begin to be measured again.

From 30 seconds, the parent continues to increase the amount of time for the child's time-out until the child is up to one minute. Then the parent increases by 30-second intervals every two or three days until the child is at the standard time-out amount, which is three minutes for a three-year-old, four minutes for a four-year-old, and so on.

Another point to consider is the time-out chair itself. Choose a chair that has no arms, no cushions, and is high enough that the child cannot touch the floor with his feet. Here are the reasons. You do not want to battle with him to keep him from lying down in the chair. You do not want him to become passive-aggressive toward you, and fall asleep in time-out to show you how ineffective you are. You do not want him to be able to easily run off. A good old-fashioned kitchen chair works well. It can also be easily moved from room to room to make it more convenient for you at various times. Choose your time-out chair wisely.

Another consideration, do not let him choose the chair, "No, mommy. I want that chair instead." There is a spark of defiance here, and that is exactly what needs to be extinguished. Instead you say, "No, Johnny. Mommy said this chair." Then you stick to it.

When time-out is used for the first time, children may think that it is a game. They may laugh and try to charm. They may even do the time-out perfectly the first time or two. Then they will get tired of this "game," and refuse to comply. That is when they discover that this is not a game. It is a requirement. It is at this point that some parents move from their rightful place as king or queen of the home, to court jester. Sometimes, we mothers get confused as to our role. We think that it is our job to keep everyone in the house happy. Putting a child into time-out makes the child unhappy. We may think, "I am a bad mom, because my child is unhappy right now, and I am causing it."

We parents forget that our children are responsible for making their own decisions. Our child is in time-out, not because we placed him there. No, he is in time-out because he made a bad choice. We are just executing discipline that had been established earlier. We do not cause the time-out—the child causes it. We simply cause the natural consequence to ensue.

Think for a moment about being in junior high or high school. You had different kinds of teachers. Right? And do you remember how there was always a first-year teacher who wanted to be a friend to her students. She wanted to be a popular teacher, so she thought she would do this by keeping everyone happy. Soon no one was happy. The class was running over her. She was whining and begging for cooperation. She was not happy, not popular, and certainly not respected by her students.

Now think about that other teacher. Remember the one who was strict, but fair. She demanded much from her students, and they delivered. How well her students did in class mattered to her, but she allowed students to fail if that was what they chose. She placed the "F" on the report card, but she did not cause the child to fail. The child caused his own failure. She expressed disappointment at the student's decision to fail, but not anger. She still cared about each student, no matter how well that student chose to do in her class. She was popular and respected.

What is the difference in these two teachers? Think about this and really understand it, because this is the goal I am working toward with the parents who come to me for help. Take on the aura of the second teacher. Be in charge. Be matter-of-fact. Be fair. Be consistent. Do not give in. Know that if you give in, you are relinquishing some of the respect that your child had for you before you caved.

EFFECTIVE TIME OUTS | 21

There is another down side to giving in. When you give in to your child, when you let her out of punishment or off of grounding early, you give her a direct message—you are a failure. It's as if you are saying, "You just can't do the hard stuff, so I'm going to have to rescue you."

When a child gets rescued time and time again, she feels weaker and weaker. Let her do the hard stuff sometimes. Let her complete the grounding. Let her do the time out. Let her miss the party because she didn't finish cleaning her room.

There is something important that goes on inside the mind of a child who is going through a natural consequence. It is called "experience." The child is gaining valuable experience. Lessons are being learned. Future behavior is being altered and improved. *In the long run*, things will be better for both you and your child, although it may not be seen in the present moment.

Another mistake that moms sometimes make is to whine at her child. "We have to sit in time out now. Come on, honey, we can do it. Please. Let's sit here with our hands on our knees. See how Mommy is sitting. Mommy will do it with you. Okay? Please?"

First of all, it is a mistake to say "we" when you mean "you." *We* are not sitting in time-out. *He* is. He is the one who mis-behaved. He needs to take responsibility for his mistakes. It is unhealthy for you to share the blame with him. Do you want him blaming you for his mistakes when he is a teenager? That is where you are headed by using the word "we" when you mean "you." Making a child responsible for his own mistakes is the beginning of making him responsible for himself.

Secondly, don't beg, order. You are the queen or king, re-member? Tell him what is expected. Demand that he obey immediately. Give a consequence when he does not—end of discussion. Use your "mommy voice" or your "daddy voice." That voice is direct, anger-free, has no hint of begging in it, and is delivered with the expectation that the command will be obeyed.

Now let's look at an example of something you might instruct your young child to do, and then we will follow it through. Let us say that you have given the command, "Come here." After giving the command, you count inside your head—not out loud—to three. If action has not begun by the time you get to three, you say, "Now you will have to do a time-out because you did not do what I told you to do."

Once you begin to move toward your child, the child cannot suddenly decide to comply and get out of the consequence. Otherwise, your child will learn that he does not even have to attempt to obey you until you begin to get up. For the child to suddenly comply because the parent is on the way to discipline the child is actually an act of defiance within the child. Therefore, once you act (get up, start walking toward the child, etc.), it is too late for the child to begin to obey. Even once you *begin* to get up, it is too late. The child gets a time-out for not obeying immediately.

Then as soon as the time-out has been served, you again give the command that had been ignored earlier, which was, "Come here." If the child once again refuses to obey or dawdles in complying with the request, another time-out is earned. This continues until the child immediately does as he is told.

You are taking back the power your child has had, power over you. You are also taking back control. So what control does your child still possess? He does have control—control over how long his time-out will be. You will begin measuring time toward his time-out when he is sitting still with his hands on his knees. There should be no look of defiance on his face. He cannot cry, talk, or make any kind of noise or movement. If he does, you tell him that you now must start his time over.

Finally, choose the setting for the time out. An Effective Time-Out (ETO) is not served in view of a television. Either go to a different room to administer the ETO, or turn off the television and discipline the child. No program is more important than what you are doing with your child. Furthermore, any toy or snack that the child is holding when he goes into time-out is put aside and will be returned once the time-out is finished.

Finally, if there are other people around, you will always take the chair and the child into a separate room. An audience can keep a strong-willed child's ego going for a long time. He does not want there to be witnesses to his abdication from his throne. Strong-willed children work best with an authority figure when it is one-on-one.

What You Do When Your Child is in Time-Out

Here is something that is very important: Do not give your child a command when he is in time-out. That will offer him the opportunity to be defiant toward you, and he is already in time-out, so what can you do about another episode of defiance? You cannot do anything. Therefore, instead of giving a command in the form of an imperative sentence, use a declarative sentence and give him some information. For instance, instead of saying, "Put your hands on your knees," (a command), say "When you put your hands on your knees, I will start timing you" (information).

The difference between these two is extremely important. We are working to help the child understand that when you tell him to do something, he has to do it. If you tell him to do something while he is in time-out (such as to put his hands on his knees), and he refuses to do it, what can you do? He is already in time-out. Adding more time to his time-out is not the answer. Therefore, instead of giving him a command that will offer him an opportunity to defy you, simply give him information. To do this, start with the word "when."

"When you put your hands on your knees, I will begin counting down your time," you say. Then you do not begin timing him until he has his hands on his knees.

If your child demands to be let out of her time-out so she can take care of some need, do not fall for this. If you do, that "need"

24 | CREATING CALM FROM CHAOS

will crop up every single time she has a time-out, and once again she has control over you. Therefore, while she is in time-out, much of what you say to her begins with the word "when."

> When you put your hands on your knees, time will start.
> When you finish your time-out, you can go to the bathroom.
> When you finish your time-out, you can get a drink.
> When you finish your time-out, I will give you a tissue.
> When you finish your time-out, I will hold you (or hug you).

As you can see, the message is clear—nothing will get you out of doing this time-out. Of the hundreds of children with which we have worked at Tender Hearts Child Therapy Center, many have told their mothers that they needed to go to the bathroom, yet none have actually wet their pants in the time-out chair. Now, if a child would wet his pants, the parent would simply finish the time-out, and then allow the child to change his clothes. Again, nothing should interrupt the time-out experience.

Many times children take off their shoes in protest while in time-out. Simply gather the shoes without emotion and tell the child that when time-out is completed she can have her shoes back. Often she yells that she wants her shoes back right now. When you do not give in, and you insist that she must wait until she completes her time-out to get her shoes back, the shoes will no longer come off. If on the other hand, she starts taking off her shoes, and you say, "Now don't take your shoes off!" Ha, she's got you! She is going to take off those shoes as a protest of this time-out thing you've started with her. Nothing will stop her now!

Remember; do not give him a command while he is in time-out. That is an invitation for disobedience. He is already angry and looking for a way to get back at you. If you give him a command, you have handed him the ammunition for which he has been looking. Start your communication with the word "When." By doing so, you do not afford him the opportunity to disobey you.

Now, let's say that you are trying to put him into time-out, and he keeps getting down. The temptation is to hold him in the chair. But how is he making the choice to give in to your authority if he is not given a choice? He has to make the choice to obey you. He has to make the choice to stay in the chair until his time-out is complete. So continue putting him back into the time-out chair and immediately releasing your hold on him.

In fact, if he is immediately trying to get off the chair, you need to try to catch him on his way down. Definitely do not let him get out of your reach, which would require you to chase him. That will be so much fun for him that he is refreshed and good for another 30 minutes of battle. Instead you should catch him on the way down from the chair, and put him back on it, then immediately release your hold on him. Of course after a while, he will begin to stiffen up, and it is a struggle to sit him down, but you do, time and time again.

Like I said earlier, the record is 110 times before the child gave in to the parent's authority. Count this as your workout and skip your pilates for the day. Additionally, do not slam your child onto the chair. Put the child on the chair in your normal and gentle fashion, without any chance for injury. It is not the force of being put on the chair that will deter the child from getting up again. It is the realization of the child that if he gets up, he will be set back down, time and time again. At this point, one of two things will happen. Optimally, your child will decide that none of his usual moves are working, and that the only way he can get out of trouble is to sit quietly in the chair. At the point where he becomes quiet and stops fighting you, he may continue to refuse to put his hands on his knees. Actually, this is the common order of things.

If he is sitting quietly but refusing to put his hands on his knees, his message to you is, "Okay, I'll do part of what you want, but I am not going to do everything you want." Since you, as the parent, need complete control in your house, you tell him calmly that he has made a good choice to sit quietly, and that

26 | CREATING CALM FROM CHAOS

as soon as he further decides to put his hands on his knees, you will count to ten, and then he can get down. Then you wait. You do not beg. You do not say, "Put your hands on your knees." What do you say? Right! "*When* you put your hands on your knees time will start." He may wait another 30 minutes or so before he complies and places his hands on his knees. That is okay. This is the control you are allowing your child— control over how long his time-out is. He will give himself the amount of time in time-out that he needs. So you wait.

How Important is it for my Child to Put Hands on Knees?

I have had some parents to ask, "Well, at least he is sitting now. Does he have to put his hands on his knees?" If he is refusing to put his hands on his knees, what message is he giving you? Isn't he being defiant toward you by refusing this simple request? If you let him off from this requirement, what is the message to him? "You win. You've got me. You're the boss." Or you may be giving him the message, "Putting your hands on your knees is too hard for you. I will have to rescue you from doing something so difficult for you, and just let you off the hook. You're not smart enough to figure out how to do it." Neither message is good for your child.

Is putting his hands on his knees too hard physically for your child? No, but it may be difficult mentally, because by complying with your request, he is relinquishing some of his power back to you. This is power he does not want to relinquish. This is power that he must relinquish.

How do you know that your child has too much power in the family? Look at how you feel. Do you often feel helpless when you are dealing with your child? Do feelings of hopelessness wash over you as you try to get your child to comply with your requests, and he refuses? If you do, that is because your child has taken away some of your power. This is power that you *need* as a parent, and power that he *does not need* as a child.

It is best for both of you, as well as for the family, if you take back that power and allow him the amount of power that a child his age needs, (which actually is very little), and give yourself the amount of power you need as a parent (which is a lot). You make this acquisition by forcing him to comply with your command of putting his hands on his knees while he is in time-out. That is the pathway for this exchange of power. Getting the power to the rightful owner (you) will do the most good for the entire family.

Therefore, the answer to the question, "Does he have to put his hands on his knees?" is an emphatic "Yes!" Making him put his hands on his knees is crucial. It makes all the difference in the world. When he finally conforms, and he will, he has just given up a lot of that power. You both feel better for it. He leaves time-out less defiant, and he is usually good for a while, instead of leaving the time-out chair to immediately do something else he knows he is not supposed to do.

Keep in mind that this new form of discipline will take much of your time for the first week or even two. But after only two weeks, the child is usually compliant. Then the threat of a time-out causes instant conformity. At this time, when the time-outs are administered they are usually done quickly— one minute per age of the child. Once in awhile, the child will test you to see if the boundaries still hold. I think of this as their Red Rover times. If you are familiar with the children's game, Red Rover, you know how this metaphor unfolds. Two teams of children stand facing each other. Each team is holding hands to create a boundary or fence of sorts. One team talks among themselves and decides which member of the opposing team they will request. Once decided, they chant, "Red Rover. Red Rover. Send Suzy right over." Little Suzy then drops the hands of her teammates, and runs with all her might toward, what she decides to be, the weakest link of their chain. If she breaks through, she is allowed to choose one opposing team member to join her team. If she cannot break their boundary, she must join the opposing team. We parents must

28 | CREATING CALM FROM CHAOS

hold our boundaries tight and not allow our strong-willed children to break through the limits we have set.

During these first two weeks, and especially the first couple of days, it will be difficult to keep from falling back on old habits of discipline. The child is refusing to sit in the chair, or is sitting but refuses to put her hands on her knees. It is tempting to spank her to get compliance or to spank her and get the discipline over with, if spanking had been the norm before embarking on this new Effective Time-Out. After all, a 5-second spanking is less time-consuming for you as the parent than monitoring a 5-minute time-out.

Keep in mind that spanking was not working. That is why you are doing something different. Resist the temptation to fall back on old, familiar paths, remembering that they did not lead you to where you needed to go. Take a deep breath, lower your voice to a whisper, and continue working on the Effective Time-Out. The child will comply. She really will. You just have to outlast her. You can do that. Then the message to the child is: This new way of doing discipline is taking longer, but you are worth my time. What a great message to give your child! Hold on to the knowledge that in a couple of weeks, your total time involved in discipline will actually be less than before you embarked on this new method of discipline, because your child will be compliant more often.

What Happens if my Child Hits Me or Calls Me Names?

Earlier I said there were two things that could happen. Besides making the decision to surrender to your authority (the desired outcome), he could decide to raise the stakes. He could begin disrespecting you with either his words or his fists. He may begin hitting, biting, kicking, or calling you names. All of these are totally inappropriate behaviors that cannot be tolerated.

If you allow him to hit you when he is two just because you think it doesn't matter since it doesn't hurt you that much, then you are setting a terrible precedent. What this act of physical or verbal aggression does is to create a learning experience—a wrinkle in his brain (literally). What he learns: I can hit my mom (or dad) when I am mad. That wrinkle will still be there when he is 16. Most children will try to hit their parents when they are small. Create a brain wrinkle with the lesson that he cannot disrespect his mother or father without a very undesirable consequence. That consequence will be explained in chapter four.

CHAPTER FOUR:
THE SAFETY HOLD

If you have started to put your child in time-out, and he disrespects you in any way, (hits, kicks, calls a name, curses, says you stink, etc.), then the time-out goes to the next level. You inform your child that he has made a bad choice, that he does not hit (or kick, etc.) his Mommy (or Daddy), and then take him over to the place where you will do a safety hold.

Usually the need for the safety hold is greatest during the first week that you begin to use the Effective Time-Out. Most often, parents will find that the safety hold is not even necessary during the second week. However, it may have to be revisited periodically as the need arises, up until your child is about six or seven. Deciding to stop use of the safety hold really depends on the size of your child, your size, and how physically healthy you are. No one should get hurt in the safety hold. If you are trying to restrain a child who is almost as strong as you are, someone could get hurt. That is why I give the rule of thumb that the safety hold is useful for children from age two through about six years of age.

For the safety hold, chose a wall against which you can sit (this will help support your back). Sit with your back against that wall. Open your legs and have your child to sit between your legs facing the same way that you are. Either each of your legs goes over each of his legs, or you can cross your legs around your child. Crossing your legs works best with smaller children. Then you cross his arms in front of him, and your arms are *not* crossed. You hold his hands at his side. (Refer to the illustrations).

THE SAFETY HOLD | 33

There are two reasons that you hold his *hands* and not his forearms. First of all, you could leave bruising on his forearms with your fingertips. Hands are tougher parts of the body and

34 | CREATING CALM FROM CHAOS

are less likely to bruise. Secondly, by putting your hands over his hands, and placing them down at his sides, he cannot reach your hands in order to bite them. It is safer for both of you.

Remember this important fact—the safety hold is just that—safe. It is not meant to hurt the child in any way. Do not use the safety hold if you are angry and unable to maintain your cool throughout the hold. (Complete an anger management course before you even begin the use of the Effective Time-Out. These courses are available at most counseling centers).

You now hold the child and tell him that when he calms down and is quiet while you count to ten, you will let go of him and then he can get into the time-out chair to finish his time-out because he threw his toy at his brother (or whatever his offense). It is important throughout this discipline event that you remind your child why he is in time-out and why he is in the safety hold. Talk about the two bad choices he made. For example, you might say, "You have to be in this safety hold because you hit Mommy when Mommy was putting you into the time-out chair. You had to go into the time-out chair because you threw the toy at your brother. You made two bad choices and that is why you are in the safety hold." Even though he may be yelling, talk quietly and calmly. He can still hear you over his own voice. Your mouth is close to his ear, so you can easily speak softly to him, which helps to calm him.

Your child will protest. He will struggle, scream, and cry. He may call you names, beg for you to let him go, or try to bargain with you. You must remain firm. He has to be quiet and still while you count to 10. This is what is best for your child. What you are doing is causing a readjustment in his thinking. For your child to try to hurt you or call you names means your child thinks he has enough power to overpower you. That is not true, and it is mentally unhealthy for him to think that he has that much power or that his caregiver is such a weakling. He cannot be allowed to get away with that line of thinking. By changing his thinking now, your life with him when he is a teenager will be much better (notice, I did not say it would be easy, but it will be better).

I have read that strong-willed children are easier as teenagers than compliant children. I think that is true in some ways, but I have found in raising two strong-willed children, that they were a challenge right up to the day they became adults, and beyond.

Now, let's look at the safety hold. The first time you use this safety hold, it will take about an hour or more before your child submits to your authority and decides that he will complete his time out. If you have a truly gifted strong-willed child, it may take longer. The important thing is that you see it through. Do not start this unless you are going to finish. Otherwise, it serves no purpose except to totally irritate your child. You do not want to irritate your child. You simply want to readjust his irrational thinking. This technique will accomplish that purpose.

In fact, there are five messages delivered to your child when you use the safety hold:

1. *If you don't control yourself, I will TOTALLY control you.* The child needs to learn self-control. It may seem odd that you teach a child self-control by totally controlling him, but that is what works. The child wants to control everyone around him. He does that by not controlling himself and by following his own impulses. Everyone around him begins to give in to him. I have seen many families where older children are expected to give the younger child their toys, their candy, whatever he wants, just to keep him from throwing a fit. Then they wonder why they have so many problems with sibling rivalry. What you are reinforcing to your strong-willed child when you use the safety hold is that he is responsible to control himself, even during those times that he does not get his way. Once he learns how to control himself, he will be less likely to try to exert his power outside of himself.

36 | CREATING CALM FROM CHAOS

2. *You are worth my time.* It would be so much faster to just spank you, or to close you in your room for five minutes, but you are worth all this time and effort because you are important to me.

3. *You can give your child some good messages.* Having your child in the safety hold affords you a captive audience (no pun intended). You can whisper *to* him some important messages in a calm and quiet manner while you are holding him. Your mouth is very close to his ear. Even if he is yelling and screaming, he will still hear your words. Some important messages that would benefit your child are as follows:

    a. *I love you*—the most important message for a child to hear. I love you, and that is why I am working here to help you learn how to make good choices. However, this is not the time usually to kiss him. Kissing is a form of positive reinforcement. Just like you would not give him candy while he is in the safety hold, you will not kiss him. You just need to reassure him of your love.

    b. *You're strong, but I am stronger.* This is a very important message to give to your strong-willed child. There are two reasons your child needs to hear this message. First of all, your strong-willed child has the mistaken belief that he can overpower you. He needs the message that he cannot overpower or bully you. He is a child and you are his parent. He must submit to your authority and you will not submit to him. The second reason your child needs to hear that you are stronger than him is that your child wants to know that he is being cared for and protected by a very strong person. It makes him feel safe that you are even stronger than him. He thinks, "Wow! I have a really strong person taking care of me! I am safe."

THE SAFETY HOLD | 37

    c. *Mommy (or Daddy) is the boss.* Children need to be reminded of this fact, especially if they have been able to garner some of the power in the family.

    d. *You need to make better choices.* Be certain to separate the acts from the child. In other words, he is always a good boy. He is just a good boy who sometimes makes bad choices. Alternately, he is a good boy who sometimes makes good choices. His choices are just that—choices. Being a good boy is WHO he is. By separating his actions from him, he can better establish his identity as a good person at this critical time in the development of his identify. You want that core belief that he is a good person to be the foundation on which he builds the rest of his identity.

4. *Your child has the opportunity to vent strong feelings.* The safety hold allows your child the *opportunity* to vent his anger and frustrations. Who doesn't feel better after a good cry? When he has completed this safety hold, he will be calmer and more centered.

5. *The safety hold allows you the opportunity to hold your child.* What better place for your child to have a "break-down" than in the arms of the person who *loves* him the most in the world? This is actually a bonding time. You are going through this together. You can be calm and nurturing as you help him to let go of his misguided belief that he is in charge of the world.

During this safety hold, he may say several things that need to be addressed. If he says that he needs to go to the bathroom, you say, "When we finish here, and then you do your time-out in the chair, you can go to the bathroom."

Only once did a child wet his pants during the safety hold, and he was a 2-year-old going through potty training. Once the child saw that Grandfather (his primary caregiver) was not allowing him out even after he wet his pants, he submitted to the authority of his grandfather. He calmly sat while Grandfather did a slow count to ten, then he hopped up onto the time-out chair and placed his hands on his knees for the allotted time. When the child realizes that *nothing* is going to get him out of completing the task you have set before him, he will decide to comply with your instructions.

The same is true for needing a drink, or being hungry. Start with that important word—*when*. When you are quiet and calm while I count to ten, then I will let you up so you can finish your time-out in the chair. Then you can get a drink OR then we will go get some lunch, etc.

If he takes off his shoes, simply push them aside and tell him he can have them back after he has been calm and quiet while you count to ten and after he completes his time in the time-out chair. When he does complete the safety hold and the time-out, hand him his shoes.

If your child is able to put his shoes on by himself, even if it takes longer than when you do it, then do not put your child's shoes back on for him. Yes, he seems a little pitiful at this moment when he has finished his time out, but resist the temptation to fall back into being his servant. Handing him his shoes instead of putting them on for him gives the important message: You decided to take these off, so you will need to take the time to put them back on. This demonstrates to your child that there are natural consequences for actions. It is another important learning moment for your child.

What can I Expect in Doing the Safety Hold?

I will give you a typical scenario of a safety hold so you will have an idea of what to expect.

Three-year-old Carson hits his sibling. Mom says, "Carson, when you hit, you sit. Go to the time-out chair. He refuses. Mom picks him up and sets him down in the time-out chair. He jumps down. She does it again. He again jumps down.

THE SAFETY HOLD | 39

She continues to catch him as he is sliding off the chair, and to set him back onto the chair. He then goes to his next effort. He stiffens his body, and she has to work to get him set back down. She is careful to not hurt him during this time. She helps him to sit, and he finds himself back on his chair. He is angry. He kicks his mother. At this point, she says, "You don't kick Mommy. Now you have to go to the safety hold."

Mom picks up Carson and takes him over to the wall where she sits to do the safety hold. (With a larger child, the parent may pull him by the hand over to the safety-hold area). She sits down, places him in front of her. She may struggle with Carson to get him positioned, but she reminds herself that it is crucial to not make any moves that would harm Carson. Again, the time-out and the safety hold are never supposed to hurt.

Throughout the safety hold experience, Carson may periodically be able to work loose a leg, and mom will calmly reposition it back into the hold. If Carson says he is being hurt, Mom reminds herself that sometimes children say they are being hurt as a way to make mom let go. Still, mom checks over their positions to make sure that Carson is not being hurt. Carson will cry. He probably will scream and may curse, if that has been his angry response in the past.

Mom takes some deep breaths to keep herself calm. She reassures her child that WHEN he calms down, she will count to 10, and then he can get up and go to the time-out chair to finish his time-out for hitting his brother. She reminds him that he kicked her, and that is why he is in the safety hold. Carson goes from crying, to being angry with his mother, to begging her to let go. She gently reminds him that once he is quiet and still, she will count to 10, and then he can go to the time-out chair.

When Carson quiets, she asks, "Carson, are you ready for me to begin counting?" He must say, "Yes." He cannot just nod. A verbal response is more of a commitment than a nod. Let's say that he nods. Mom responds, "I need you to say yes." He growls, and begins struggling again. Finally when she asks him if he is ready for her to count, he says, "Yes."

40 | CREATING CALM FROM CHAOS

Mom begins counting, and Carson grunts loudly in anger. Mom stops counting and says, "You are not ready yet. We will wait until you are ready to be still and to be quiet." He immediately begins struggling against her and yelling. She waits. After a minute or two, he quiets, and she asks him, "Are you ready for me to count?" He says, "No!" at which point she simply and calmly says, "Then we will wait."

Carson begins to realize that mom is not falling for any of his usual ploys. She seems to mean business this time. Allowing Carson to decide when she starts counting, allows Carson control, and it is all the control he needs to be given in this circumstance. How long he will be in the safety hold is entirely up to him. To get out of the safety hold, he must comply with the instructions of his parent.

While Carson is in the safety hold, she gives him the good messages that were suggested earlier. She tells him she loves him. She reminds him that she is the boss. He may even try to argue, screaming out that he is the boss. She doesn't fall into arguing with him while he is in a safety hold. She simply says, "When you decide that Mommy is the boss, you will be making a good choice." Then she does not respond further even if he tries to argue with her. When he struggles against her physically, she says, "You are strong, but I am stronger." She talks simply and matter-of-factly to him about choices concerning hitting his sibling, and what he could have done differently. She does not display anger.

When mom feels frustrated, she takes a few deep breaths and reminds herself that this present behavior is being extinguished, and soon Carson's behavior will be better. When he is loud while she is talking, she simply puts her mouth next to his ear and whispers. Her quiet talk and whispers help to calm Carson. Sometimes she is quiet and allows him to yell and scream in his frustration at having his power taken back by his parent. She basks in the knowledge that this transfer of power is going to help the whole family to better function.

From this point there are several ways this encounter could go. Usually the actions mentioned above will be repeated over and over. Mom will respond the same way each time. Eventually, he will decide that he is ready for her to count. It is okay for Mom to ask from time to time, "Are you ready for me to start counting?" This reminds him that there is one way and only one way out of his present predicament. He must comply with his mother.

Mom must resist the temptation to just begin counting without him giving the verbal reply of yes. Remember, our purpose in doing this safety hold is two-fold. Yes, it is for punishment because he kicked his mother. However, it is also to get rid of the defiance he has been displaying to the world. If you just begin counting without having him to verbally say, "yes," he will likely hold on to some of his defiance and you will experience a worse time at the time-out chair in a minute or two. Require that he say "Yes" when he is ready for you to count. He WILL say that he is ready eventually, and then will stay quiet and still while Mom slowly counts to 10. I promise; it will happen. Just hang in there.

Mom slowly counts to ten, and this is serving a purpose of its own. The slow counting has a calming effect on the child. The world is becoming predictable again. Two comes after one, and then there is three. Yes, I know what to expect, he thinks. There is a feeling of safety that begins to grow inside of him as his world becomes predictable once more.

Once she has reached 10, Mom does not release her hold on Carson immediately. She first asks, "Now, if I let you go, will you go straight to the time-out chair? You need to sit in the time-out chair with your hands on your knees." If Carson indicates in any way that he will not do this, Mom says, "Well, then, we will sit here a while longer until you are ready to sit in the time-out chair." Again, this is giving Carson control: control over how long the safety hold lasts.

Once he agrees to go to the time-out chair, Mom releases him, and then watches him carefully. The time-out chair should be just a few steps away. If he dawdles at all, she says, "I don't think you are ready yet," and she pulls him back down into the safety hold again. What she needs from him at this point is total compliance. She wants him to go straight to the chair and get up onto the chair. Anything less requires another safety hold.

Usually, once Carson realizes he must go straight to the chair or he will find himself back in the safety hold, he will comply. And most often, once he complies in going straight to the chair, he further complies in immediately placing his hands on his knees. His time-out begins, and ten seconds later it is all over.

However, if mom has been too easy on him in the safety hold, allowing him to grunt while she counted to ten, for example, then he is returning to the time-out chair with some defiance still showing. He may not immediately place his hands on his knees. This is still a requirement for the time-out to begin. He may try to wait mom out, and when he sees it is not working, he will surrender to her authority and put his hands on his knees.

On the other hand, he may continue to struggle with her and end up back in the safety hold another time. The scenario depends on how strong-willed your child is, and it also depends on how strong-willed you are. It is important that your will outlasts the will of your child. You are more determined that he surrender his authority back to you, than he is determined to retain the authority he has garnered from you.

You may think this whole scenario is a little harsh. I assure you, it is not. Time-outs are not cruel punishment. You have a strong-willed child who requires extra work to get him to the point of being able to do a time-out. Your ultimate goal is to have a child who will do his time-out when you tell him to. That goal is a good goal for any parent.

Earlier I had talked about Stevie. At that first session with Stevie and his parents, I told Dad that eventually he would be able to walk out of the room for a few seconds, and return to find Stevie still sitting in the chair with his hands on his knees. Dad looked at me incredulously. When this very thing happened just three weeks later, Dad excitedly told me about it, saying that he had never thought it would ever happen. He was pleased with his child and with himself as a parent.

There are a few things you need to keep in mind as you do the safety hold. Just as he did with the time-out chair, your child will look for reasons to get out of the safety hold. He needs a drink of water, to go to the bathroom, etc. Just as you do with the time-out, you do with the safety hold. You do not allow the safety hold to be interrupted. When communicating with your child while he is in the safety hold, remember to begin your communication with that all-important word. What is it? Right! The word "when." Only now there are more steps before he is free to return to his play or to whatever he is asking to do. "When you are calm until I count to 10, then I will let you out of this safety hold, and you can finish your time-out in the time-out chair. Then you can go to the bathroom."

Furthermore, you do not allow yourself to be interrupted. The phone can ring, and you remind yourself that you can return a call to that person after you finish this most important task of getting control of your child. Nothing will interrupt you in this all-important pursuit. When you display this attitude, your child comes to realize the importance of what is taking place.

"Hold fast. Hold firm." That is your mantra as you perform the safety hold. It has two applications. You can apply it to the physical side of what you are doing with your child. You can also apply it to the mental side of what you are doing to remind yourself to keep on, to persevere. Consistency and persistency are the two keys to making this method work. The first two days are the worst. After that, you will wonder why you didn't start it sooner.

CHAPTER FIVE:
THE SURRENDER (The Child's—Not Yours)

There will be times throughout this new course of discipline when you might think, "This is not working. I might as well give up. She will never do it. She will never put her hands on her knees for a time-out." This chapter is for you during those times.

When parents are in our therapy center, doing their first Effective Time-Out with their strong-willed child, I am able to be there with them. We are in it together. Mom or Dad is getting immediate instruction as needed, and I am the cheerleader for those moments of triumph. I also serve as an encourager for those moments of discouragement. I cannot be there with you, unless, of course, you want to call and make an appointment at our center in Jackson, Missouri. However, if you cannot make the trip, then re-read these past few chapters over and over. This book is short. You should re-read it several times before you even begin to use the Effective Time-Outs. The re-reads will not take long. Then continue to re-read it throughout that first week.

You have the nuts and bolts of how to use the Effective Time-Out method. The rest will have to come from inside of you. Before you begin this new course of discipline, make certain that you understand the theory, the foundation, the reason for what you are doing. Let me help you with that. Many times strong-willed children have been able to gain power, more power than they know what to do with. As they display power, parents try to appease them, and inadvertently give them even more power with each encounter. The Effective Time-Out method with the child putting her hands on her knees allows you to take back all the power that your child has taken from you. It is a way to force the child to comply with your instructions.

There will be times at the beginning when you think this method is not working and you just want to give up on it. I encourage you to give it a week of total consistency and persistency. If the Effective Time-Out method has made no difference or very little difference in your child's behavior, you probably need to take your child to a children's therapist for an assessment. But give this your best shot, as if it were a last resort.

I had a mother to come in with her out-of-control three-year-old, whom I will call Derek. After I talked to her about the use of the Effective Time-Out and the use of the Safety Hold, Derek defied her, and she decided to put her newfound knowledge to work. The problem was that she had been at the hospital all night with a younger child who was ill, and she had come straight from the hospital, swinging by to pick up Derek at the babysitter's in order to keep the appointment at our center. She was exhausted.

She had tried to put Derek into time-out, and he retaliated by kicking her. She went to the Safety Hold, as he struggled against her. He began calling her names and trying to bite her. After a short time of putting up with this abuse, she suddenly let go of Derek and began to sob. She said, "I just can't do it. I am just going to send him to live with his dad. I can't do this. He won't mind me. It is just too hard." I observed mom who was frustrated and exhausted. Her resolve was gone. Her physical exhaustion had sapped her of her mental endurance, and it does take mental endurance to see the Safety Hold to the end.

I looked over to Derek. He looked so little as he was lying cross-wise on the couch in our Family Therapy Room. He was on his tummy, his knees bent, and his feet in the air behind him. He was quiet and his big, brown eyes looked confused as he watched his mother. My heart went out to this child. If mom followed through with this threat to ship him off to his dad's, the message to him is, "You are a bad boy. You are so bad that I don't want you anymore. I am sending you away from me."

Don't get me wrong. I see nothing wrong with a dad raising a child. I see many instances when the father is better equipped to raise the child. But no child needs to be sent to live with the other parent because he or she is "bad." If the child interprets that action as being unloved by a parent, the child could believe himself to be unlovable by anyone. After all, if a parent cannot love you, you must not deserve to be loved, the child may decide. I feared these circumstances were going to damage Derek's self-esteem.

I encouraged the mother to wait a week and then to bring Derek back to our center. I reminded her that she was too tired to have started the Effective Time-Out method today. She agreed to come back in a week.

When this mother returned the next week, she was rested and calm. She said she had actually started using the Effective Time-Out and the Safety Hold the day following her appointment with me. She said it had made a big difference. She explained how she had been determined to give the method her best shot, knowing she would send him to live with his dad if the method did not work. She was surprised, she said, at how well Effective Time Out worked and how quickly the changes came. She smiled and whispered to me, "I like Derek now. I haven't felt that I even liked him for a long time because he was so mean to me. I always loved him, but I also like him now. It feels good."

48 | CREATING CALM FROM CHAOS

There is nothing more wonderful than when the child surrenders authority to the parent. When that defiant little child suddenly takes a deep breath and then puts her hands on her knees, remaining still and calm for the full count of ten, I cannot tell you how wonderful that feels to me. New possibilities arise in the hearts and minds of the parents. I know that this family is well on their way to being more functional and happier. I applaud the parent and the child, and richly praise both of them.

In the therapy session, offering this praise to the child is often my first interaction with the child since the parent and child entered the family therapy room. I have only dealt with the parent, telling the parent what to say to the child and instructing the parent on what to do. After all, it is the parent, not I, who must be viewed by the child as being the authority figure.

The amazing part of the surrender is that the child surrenders authority to other authority figures in his or her life as well as the parents. Once the child learns the skill of self-control in order to spend less time in the time-out chair, he uses this new skill everywhere he goes. He enjoys having self-control and is sure to practice it at pre-school, in church, in a restaurant, and everywhere.

This first surrender is the most important one. The surrender of authority to you, the authority figure, is very big in the child's psyche. However, he still holds out some hope that this present discipline will be short-lived, and that his power will be restored in a few days if he makes it hard enough on his parents.

He knows that you won this battle, but he still hopes to win the war. He still hopes that he can wear you down and regain his place as king of the household. So there will be several episodes during the first two days when you must be consistent and persistent. The child must come to understand that this new hierarchy in the family, with parents at the top of command, is here to stay. The children I have seen quickly adjusted. In fact, once they realize what is expected of them,

THE SURRENDER (THE CHILD'S—NOT YOURS) | 49

they are relieved. They come to accept their new role as a subject to the king and queen of the house. They come to appreciate that life is now predictable and they know what will happen when they break the rules.

I always tell parents as they leave our center after learning our technique and going through that first Effective Time-Out, which usually includes a Safety Hold, that they must not give the child any breaks during this first week. If they instruct their child to do something or to not do something, and the child ignores or disobeys, it is automatically a time-out. I tell the parents to not let anything slide this first week as they train the child that obedience is not optional.

I tell the parents that there may be times in the next week when they think, "Oh, I wish I hadn't told her to do that, because she is ignoring me, and now I am going to have to back up what I have said with action." It is important to back it up, though. No matter how tired or hurried you feel. You are laying the foundation for what will come next. You want good things to come next. This is quality time you are giving your child. Your child is worth it.

Many times in that initial assessment session, before I teach the Effective Time Out Method, I observe that the children are told by the parents to do something, the children ignore the parents, and the parents then ignore the child's act of disobedience. Therefore, I usually take time at the end of this first instructional session to point out specific examples to the parent of incidents in which they ignored the child's disobedience in the beginning of the session, and I will encourage the parents to follow-through if another opportunity presents itself, which it will.

I remind them of the persistence part of the commitment. I prepare the parents for the fact that the child will be in time-out often during this first week of training. The child is going to have a rough week, and they as parents will also have a rough week, but life will continue to get better and better after this first week. I encourage them to hang in there and not cave.

CHAPTER SIX:
WHAT ABOUT MY CHILD'S SPIRIT?

In the case of Andrew mentioned in Chapter 2, Andrew's grandfather was concerned that my methods would break his spirit. I was able to assure him that if done properly, the child's spirit would not be broken. Only Andrew's misguided will that caused him to refuse to conform to authority would be broken. That, of course, is a good thing to break.

I asked the grandfather, "Do you know what will break his spirit? When he starts kindergarten and gets into trouble every day. When none of the other kindergarteners will play with him because he is always in trouble, and in kindergarten, the other children do not like the troublemaker. When he feels disliked by teachers and peers—that will break his spirit. Being forced to comply with authority will not break his spirit. It will enhance his life."

Thank goodness for Andrew's sake, his grandfather felt that my explanation made sense. He agreed to do the Effective Time-Outs with Andrew. I spoke to Grandma on several occasions thereafter, when I'd run into her in the community, and she only had praises to sing about the Effective Time-Out. She said that Andrew was doing wonderfully in kindergarten, and he was not getting into trouble. He had learned self-control and was using it at school to be successful.

Andrew's newfound success was building up his self-esteem. This is true self-esteem, not some syrupy, praise-laden round of self-esteem-building that is based on extrinsic rather than intrinsic factors. Self-esteem that wells up within the child and spills out onto her face due to her success at a difficult task, is much more real and lasting than the self-esteem that comes from a parent or teacher looking for *something* for which to praise the child. That kind of praise feels as false to the child's ears as it feels to the parent or teacher's mouth. As a teacher and as a parent, I remember seeing the confused look on the faces of children who were normally in trouble, but were now being gushed-over for some minor conformity into which they accidentally fell.

If we foster our children's ability to have self-control, we will enjoy the by-product of that, which is an elevation in their self-esteem. However, if we build up a child's self-esteem, without teaching them to have self-control, we have just created a little monster who feels he is entitled to *everything* without having earned *anything*. Teaching self-control to a strong-willed child gives that child the recipe for going far and accomplishing much in his life.

CHAPTER SEVEN:
WHAT TO DO IN PUBLIC PLACES

Strong-willed children will misbehave wherever they can get away with misbehaving. On the other hand, they will behave wherever they are forced to behave. Therefore, if you allow your child to misbehave in a particular setting, at the grocery store, for example, then you must expect misbehavior every time you take your child into that setting. A child quickly learns the outer limits of what she can get away with, and will spend much time near that boundary. Your message to your child must be: You are expected to behave no matter where I take you. A second important message: You are worth my time to help you to be the best that you can be, no matter where we are. Then prove to them by your actions that you believe in these two truths.

What to do when Shopping

First of all, before you leave for shopping, have an alternate plan that covers the scenarios that might unfold when you go to the grocery store. These are called your Plan B and

54 | CREATING CALM FROM CHAOS

Plan C. In other words, have options. Often, we as parents do not think through the what-ifs.

Of course your Plan A is that you go to the grocery store, and your child either behaves, or he responds in a positive way whenever he is corrected. You finish shopping, and you both leave the store with smiles on your faces.

Plan B is your first alternate plan. Perhaps Plan B is that if your child does not respond to your correction of him, then you will take your child to the restroom in the store. You will put a paper towel on the bathroom floor and declare it to be the time-out chair. Have the child to sit on the paper towel, knees bent, and hands on his knees. This can work if the child cooperates. If he does not, you do not want to go to a restraint in a public place. The public will not be able to understand what you are doing, and if the child screams and yells, a heroic security guard who thinks you are trying to kidnap a child could tackle you. So if the child acts aggressively during the time-out, you go to Plan C, which may mean one of several other options.

If possible, it was planned from the beginning that you and your spouse would be taking your child to the store together. That way if your child misbehaves, and then refuses to do the time-out in the restroom, then Plan C could mean that one of you will take your child to the car and the other one will finish the shopping. By the way, whoever is elected to finish the shopping should not buy the child any kind of toy or special treat. By doing so, that parent is setting himself or herself up as the "good guy," and the parent who takes the child to the car can look like the mean parent. A united front is necessary for the child to conform more quickly. Work together!

An alternate plan could also mean that you, if you are the lone shopper, will take the cart to a store employee and tell the store employee that you are sorry, but you must leave with your misbehaving child, and you will return later to finish the shopping.

You have set up this Plan C ahead of time. You know where to take your child. Someone is on stand-by. You take your child to the babysitter or grandparent who has agreed to care for the child while you finish your shopping. Then, you do the shopping on your own. Be certain your child knows that you went back to the store without him and, again, no treats or toys. In keeping with the idea that you are always on your child's side, you may want to tell your child how much you missed getting to shop with him, and to express your hope that next time there is a shopping trip, your child will be able to go with you and will conform to your requests while in the store so that you can finish the shopping together.

If you do not have someone available to watch your child while you return to the store to finish your shopping, then you simply cannot finish your shopping at this time. Take your cart to a store employee and explain that you must leave with your misbehaving child, and that you will not be back today. Then you leave the store. You will return another day to try it again.

If you can get by for a day or two without those groceries, try to have a natural consequence to occur because your child interrupted your shopping. "Well, Tommy, I knew we were out of cereal and I was planning to buy more, but I had to leave the store because you misbehaved. You'll have to eat oatmeal (or toast) today. We can try to finish shopping this evening. I hope you will not act out in the store so that we will be able to buy all the things we need, including your favorite cereal. Then you can have a better breakfast tomorrow."

At a Restaurant

Again, planning is essential. Explain to your child ahead of time exactly what is expected and what will happen if she misbehaves. Plan to do a time-out in the restroom if needed. If she refuses to do her time-out, plan to get your order as "Take Home." Talk to your child about all of this before you arrive at the restaurant.

Another trick is to plan to have a little ice cream or other treat at the end of the meal. If your child misbehaves and you have to leave, you do not order the treat as part of the "Take

56 | CREATING CALM FROM CHAOS

Home" order. I do not consider the treat to be a bribe. Often we have dessert when we eat out. Warn the child before you even arrive at the restaurant, that if you have to get a "Take Home" order then it will not include dessert. Then it is a natural consequence to the misbehaving. The child *chose* to not have ice cream when she *chose* to misbehave in the restaurant.

At a Relative's or a Friend's House

It is important to do the time-out in a private place so that it only involves you and your child. If a strong-willed child has an audience, he can keep his defiance going and going for hours.

Take the time-out chair to a private area, a bedroom, for example, and do the time-out there. You will deliver a message to your child: You are taking me away from my visit with my friends/relatives, but you and your behavior are important to me.

This time-out will take less of your actual time than if you have an out-of-control child that you constantly have to discipline. It will also help you to feel like the competent parent that you are. You will be in control of your child. Your hosts will appreciate your diligence in keeping your child from destroying their house, hurting their child, or treating them with disrespect. Your child will get those two important messages mentioned in the first paragraph of this chapter. I will repeat them here for you.

Message #1: You are expected to behave no matter where I take you.

Message #2: You are worth my time to help you to be the best that you can be, no matter where we are.

In the Car

Driving in the car is a dangerous venture in itself, but add a screaming out-of-control child, and the danger goes up exponentially. There have been car accidents caused by a disruptive child in a car. Children must learn that there is certain behavior that is expected from them when they are traveling in a car.

Let's say you are on your way someplace, and your 3-year-old begins to act-out. You give him a warning that if he doesn't behave, he will have to do a Car Time-out. If he does not heed this warning, you pull to a safe place. If it is a hot day, you find a shady spot. You can leave the car running, if it is needed for heat or for air. You get out of the car, you open his door, and you calmly tell him that he is now in time-out. You explain that when he has been quiet for three minutes then you will get back in the car and finish your trip (adjust the minutes according to their age). You leave him in his car seat. You close his door.

Then you get the magazine, you know the one that you never have time to read, but which you now keep in the car for just such times as these, when you can have some time for yourself. It is better to leave the car running so you have heat or air, and that way the windows can stay up. When the doors are closed and the windows are up, he is isolated from you, and this isolation makes it feel more like a disciplinary action to him.

Make certain that you are not accidentally locking yourself out of the car! You stay right there beside the car, but you are outside of the car and your child is inside. You may need to use your cell phone to call and say that you are going to be a little late because you have to take care of some important mommy-business. When he realizes that the only way to get you back in the car is to be quiet, he will comply. I don't necessarily recommend hands on the knees in this instance since he is, in many ways, already in a restraint. This action will give your child the message: Good behavior is expected in the car.

An alternative method for when it is raining, too hot or too cold, or if you are not comfortable outside of the car for any reason, is to stay in the car, looking through your magazine and ignoring the screams of your child. Once he is calm, you lay aside your magazine and give him your attention. You acknowledge him by saying, "I see that you are quiet now. If you sit quietly for three minutes, Mommy will start driving again. I cannot drive when you are yelling and screaming because that would be too dangerous." If he begins yelling and screaming, you pick up your magazine again and begin reading.

Eventually you will be on your way. This stop will not go on forever. Take a deep breath and know that you are doing what is best for you and your child.

In Church or Other Like Settings

I always recommend a nursery for children up to age four. However, some churches do not offer a nursery, and there are times in similar settings when the child is expected to be still and quiet.

Again, planning is very important. Have a special bag with quiet toys, stickers, a coloring sheet, or other age-appropriate items for your child. Allow some movement and wiggles by your child. Allow whispers, but not out-loud talking.

If your child becomes disruptive, take her to the restroom or other room offered by your church. Do a time-out. Discuss with her what your expectations are. Then return to the service. Repeat this as often as is necessary. If a restraint becomes necessary, you will need to take your child home. There needs to be a reward for making it through the church service and a consequence if your child does not. The reward could be choosing a restaurant for lunch after the service, for example. The consequence could be that you do not eat out, but go home for a sandwich instead. These do not need to be outlandish rewards, just something that can be repeated for three or four weeks in a row.

Once your child has been able to stay in the service for three to four weeks, this goal is met. You may still want to eat out as a family, but now you also decide where to go as a family, instead of allowing your child to choose for everyone.

CHAPTER EIGHT:
MONSTER TIME-OUTS AND TOTAL TIME-OUTS

Monster Time-Outs

There will come times when your child will defiantly do something that is blatantly against your rules. For example, he kicks a baby lying on the floor, or she darts away from you in a store or other public place while you are telling her to stop. These are not the usual misbehaviors; these are "bigger" infractions of the rules, and they require "bigger" consequences, hence the Monster Time-Out.

You do not use the Monster Time-Out until your child is well-established with the Effective Time-Out. Then you can pull this one out to show them what behaviors you consider to be essential. To do a Monster Time-Out, you simply double their time. For example, a four-year-old would get eight minutes in the Monster Time-Out using the Effective Time-Out position of hands-on-knees.

The Monster Time-Out is a rare beast. If you use the Monster Time-out too often, it loses its impact. Save it for really big misbehaviors. Once introduced, it should not be used more than once a week, if that often. Furthermore, it should not be introduced to your child until he has been doing the Effective

60 | CREATING CALM FROM CHAOS

Time-Out for at least a full month. If your three-year-old has not gotten used to doing his three-minute Effective Time-Out, he will be completely frustrated if you suddenly require a six-minute time-out. This bears repeating: Your child needs to be successfully doing his required minutes with hands-on-knees for at least a month before you introduce the Monster Time-Out to him.

Total Time-Outs

Another tool you can use is the Total Time-out. Children will misbehave at times because they are overly tired. They did not get to sleep until late the night before or they have had a more physically exhausting day than usual. If it is 30 minutes to an hour before bedtime, and you have had to discipline your child several times that evening, then you can issue *one* warning that the Total Time-Out may be necessary. After this one warning, if she does not immediately change her behavior, it is too late. Act. Again, there will be no story or other parts of her usual bedtime routine.

If you do not follow up immediately once you have issued the warning and the misbehavior has continued, then you have given this message to your child: If you don't straighten up, I'm going to threaten you again with a Total Time-out. That is weak. Take your rightful place, O Queen or King, and allow your royal subjects to fall into line! You are more powerful than you realize!

If the misbehavior continues after you have issued one warning, tell her she needs to put her pajamas on, brush her teeth, and go to bed. There will be no story or other parts of her usual bedtime routine. No doubt, she will cry and protest, but you remain firm. If she becomes physical with you or her disrespect is over-the-top, you inform her that now she must have a Safety Hold before her Total Time-out. Once she is in bed, you treat her in the same manner that you normally do for bedtime, (See Chapter 11).

When your child has had a rough evening that has caused you to constantly have to dish out discipline, then you both deserve some time away from each other. The natural consequence for her is to go on to bed and get some rest. Let her know that tomorrow is a new day, a starting-over place, and she can choose to have a better day tomorrow. Tell her you will look forward to seeing her in the morning. Give her a kiss. Leave the room. Go and get some rest for yourself. (You may need a Total Time-Out, too!)

CHAPTER NINE:
WHAT DO I DO WITH MY OTHER CHILDREN WHILE I AM TEACHING THE EFFECTIVE TIME-OUT TO MY STRONG-WILLED CHILD?

What Do I Do with My Baby?

Many times when I am counseling a mother who has an out-of-control preschooler, she also has an infant. There may be a direct correlation between the two. Mom has just gone through nine months of pregnancy. She has not been on-top-of-things with her toddler during this time of having morning sickness and then waddling around. Now she is busy with the new baby. She is up several times in the night, and she is tired through the day. She is still unable to give her best to her preschooler. Meanwhile, he has taken full advantage of having a mother who has given him a longer leash. When Mom realizes one day that she has let him go for too long, Mom may find that taking back her power is more difficult than she had realized it would be.

It is of the essence that Mom concentrate on the out-of-control child during this first week of training him on doing an Effective Time-Out. He will have most of her attention for the entire week. That is what is necessary in order for everyone in the household to have a better life.

One time, a mother came to get help with her three-year-old, (let's call him Jimmy), because she had found Jimmy standing over his infant brother's car seat with a raised knife, preparing to stab the infant. She was frantically looking for immediate help, and was sent to our office by her pediatrician. Jimmy was gifted in being strong-willed. Mom had to use the safety hold for over an hour before he surrendered his authority back to her. He finished his 10-second Effective Time-Out with his hands on his knees. Afterward, he looked like a different child. The anger was gone. He had become a child again, instead of being the ruler of his little kingdom.

When she was ready to leave, I helped her to her car by carrying the car seat with the infant in it. She opened the back door of her car and told Jimmy to get into his car seat. He jumped right into his car seat and sat calmly. Mom turned to me in disbelief. She said, "That is the first time Jimmy has ever done that. Usually I have to wrestle with him to get him fastened in. I can't believe it!" Her life changed that day for the better. So did Jimmy's and so did the baby's.

I always tell the mothers of infants that their baby is going to have a bad week. The baby will cry a lot during that first week when mom is busy working with the older child, but after that first week, the baby's whole life will be better. The baby will be in less danger and will be able to have a better relationship with his or her older sibling. No permanent damage will ensue because of this one week.

When you begin the process of giving your child a time-out, you first put the baby into a safe place. I am not a proponent of propping a baby's bottle, but if you have to prop a bottle, that is okay for this week only. Your baby will recover from having this bad week. There won't be permanent damage, and, as I stated previously, his life will be better hereafter, but your focus for this week MUST be on the older child.

If you start a time-out, and then leave your older child to care for the younger one, what is your message to that older

WHAT DO I DO WITH MY OTHER CHILDREN | 65

child? What your older child understands is, "The baby is more important than me. No matter what I do, I can't seem to get Mom's attention."

It is no wonder the older child resents the younger one. He used to have mom's full attention. Now he cannot have undivided attention for even a little while.

The first week is usually a rough week for everyone. The child who is being trained is in time-out and/or a safety hold often. Mom is having a bad week because she is constantly putting a child into time-out or doing the safety hold. And the infant is having a bad week because he is doing a lot of crying. But this is only for one week. Things will get better and better as the days go by.

What about my Younger Children who are not Infants?

If the younger sibling is not an infant, the same policy is used. Put the younger child, into a safe place and then work exclusively with the older one during those time-outs and safety holds. You can strap him into the high chair with a snack and his sippy-cup, and put him in front of Sesame Street or one of his videos so he is entertained while you are busy. I am not a proponent of doing this usually, but you may have to do this for one week while you are teaching the Effective Time-Out to your older child. If the younger child becomes unhappy and cries, then he will just have to cry for a while. Let me remind you this concentration of time going toward one child will ease after the first week.

If the other child is a twin, follow the same procedure as in the previous paragraph. You cannot have a child running around and distracting the child with whom you are working. I have seen younger siblings cry in sympathy when their older sibling is in a safety hold. Others have come over and hit the child who was in a safety hold. I once saw a three-year-old twin hit the mother who was restraining his twin. None of these scenarios is a good one. Strap these children into their

66 | CREATING CALM FROM CHAOS

high chairs, give them something to do, make sure they are safe, and then concentrate on your out-of-control child. At this point, you can only work with one child at a time. Later, you will be able to put two children into time-out at the same time. That will come once they have gone through their week of training.

What about my Older Children?

When you have older children, I recommend that you have a talk with them at the very beginning and let them know what will be expected of them if you get busy with their brother or sister. Discuss all of your particular rules beforehand so that you do not have to deal with decision-making when you are busy with your strong-willed child. The most important rule must be that they leave the room where you are working with your younger child. They are to remain out of the room until you are finished. They are not to interrupt. If they are old enough, they are to care for the other children until you are finished working with your child of focus.

Tell them what to do if the phone should ring—either let it ring without answering it or have the older child to take a message. Under no circumstances are they to bring you the phone while you are busy with this younger child. You are busy giving this child an important message: Right now, you are so very important. In fact, you are more important than anyone who could be calling me on the phone.

If the older child follows through with what you need from him, be sure to offer a round of praise. Help him to understand that his contribution is helping the family to function better and more happily. He is probably all in favor of getting the younger child under control. His life has probably been negatively affected by this out-of-control child up to this point, and he would like to have some of the attention directed back toward him at times.

CHAPTER TEN:
WHAT ABOUT DAY CARES AND SITTERS?

One child who came to see me had been kicked out of seven area day care centers. After mom began using this method at home, the child used her self-control to have better behavior in the day care setting as well. The child generalizes the use of this skill to include other places he or she frequents. Many people benefited from this one child's use of self-control that was begun in our center, practiced in the home, and used wherever the child went.

Some parents don't want to wait for the child to use their newfound ability to have self-control. They want the continuity of discipline in all the child's settings. This is strictly a choice for each parent to make. Although I do not feel it is necessary for the day care workers to use the same method that mom is using at home, if the day care workers are willing, and this is the wish of the parents, I see no harm in using it.

I had one mother who taught the Effective Time-Out and Safety Hold to her day care provider. The day care worker talked to another parent who agreed for the day care worker to begin using this method with her difficult child while he was in her day care center. The worker was pleased to find that it worked with other children in her care.

68 | CREATING CALM FROM CHAOS

One of the mothers who came to see me asked me to train her day care provider so that the method could be used with her daughter at pre-school. I was happy to do so, and it worked well for them.

I do not believe that the Effective Time-Out has to be practiced in all of a child's settings in order for it to work. The home is the main place where the Effective Time-Out needs to be instituted. What the parent is teaching is self-control. The child will happily use that newly learned skill everywhere he goes. The child enjoys having self-control and wants to practice and maintain it.

Likewise, if the child's parents are no longer married, both parents do not have to use this method in order for it to make a difference. If both parents want to use this method, that is wonderful, but if only one parent is on-board with the Effective Time-Out, it can still be a great benefit to the child. The parent who decides to employ the Effective Time-Out does so in his or her home, and that is where the positive changes will first take root. The roots will grow to encompass all settings around the child's world. It will work! I see it working every day.

CHAPTER ELEVEN:
BEDTIME

Do not make any changes to your child's bedtime routine until your child is doing his time-outs cooperatively. Then allow yourself a couple of weeks to a month in which your child is being cooperative in your now-functional family. When he does try to regain control of the family, you have the Effective Time-Out plan in place. Once everything is running smoothly and you have regained your stamina, you may feel ready for the next challenge of changing your child's bedtime to make it better fit into the family routine.

Strong-willed children are usually difficult at bedtime. Mom and Dad are often exhausted by the end of the day and are no longer up to the task of being firm. One time of "giving in" and allowing the child to lie down with the tired and sleepy parents, and a door has been opened. Now, no amount of pushing seems like enough to close that door again. Here is some help.

The First Step

First of all decide when you would like your child to go to bed. You cannot get your child to bed early and have the child

70 | CREATING CALM FROM CHAOS

to sleep late, no matter how much this scenario appeals to you. Therefore, decide what would work best in your routine. Should you get your child to bed early and then have him up early, or would it work best in your family routine if he went to bed late and then rose later in the morning. Once you have decided the goal for when your child goes to bed, you will go on to step number two, three, and four. However, you will continue to move your child's bedtime earlier and earlier, throughout this "bedtime betterment" until you reach the desired time.

Let's say that at the present time you are following the typical path of parents with a strong-willed child. That means that your child does not have a bedtime, but stays up until you go to bed. Now, let's say that your desire is for your child to go to bed at eight o'clock, which will allow you some time to do chores, prepare for the next day, and talk to your spouse.

It is important for you to ease into this new bedtime routine. For example, if your child normally is up until eleven o'clock when you go to bed, then you will need to start by putting her to bed at ten-thirty. When things are going fairly smoothly at ten-thirty, (which will probably take a couple of weeks), then move it up to ten o'clock for a week, then nine-thirty for a week. Continue moving it up in half-hour intervals, each lasting a week, until finally, your goal of eight o'clock has been reached. Remember that throughout this process, she will be getting up earlier and earlier in the mornings.

The Second Step

The second step in the bedtime process is to look at your child's usual bedtime routine. Often there is not a routine, per se. I find there are two usual paths that are often taken by parents of strong-willed children. For some parents, the child falls asleep on the living room couch while watching television. In fact, I have counseled several families in which the parents go on to bed, leaving the child awake on the couch in front of the television. For other children, the child goes to bed with the parent. Sometimes the parent has to shush the child over and over again as they work to get to sleep. Neither of these scenarios offers a healthy bedtime routine. Children like routine. In fact, they thrive on it. Decide what your routine will be.

We had the following routine with our children:

1. put on pajamas
2. brush teeth
3. get into bed
4. read a story (when I had two children, each got to choose one story)
5. say prayers
6. get tucked in
7. get a kiss
8. parent turns off light
9. parent leaves the room

After I went through these steps, my husband, being the musical parent, would come in to sing a song with our children. This bedtime routine was often my favorite time of the day. I might start the process feeling like I needed to rush it along as I thought about what I needed to do before I could go to bed. However, as the routine unfolded, my tensions would ease, and I would begin to enjoy the moment. I often found myself being totally present with my children during this time.

Your part in establishing your children's bedtime routine and, thereby, having an enjoyable bedtime with your child, is to decide what components you want to include. You can put the components you and your child choose onto a list for your child to check off, if your child likes checklists. Be aware that during this first week, you need to allow an hour from the time you begin the routine until the target time of your child being asleep. That means that if you want your child asleep by ten this first week, you will begin your bedtime routine at nine o'clock. As the routine becomes more, well, routine, it will take less and less time. In the end, your child's bedtime routine will take 20 to 30 minutes.

The Third Step

The third step is to share with your child what your expectations are. Be excited about this new bedtime routine, and explain that you are changing the way you do bedtime because it is best for your child. Prepare for this night ahead of time. For a few days before your starting date, announce to your child on several occasions that bedtime is going to change on the designated night, perhaps Friday night. Explain to your child that he has his own bedroom, and he is going to begin sleeping in his own bed. Work to make this change as exciting as possible.

If your budget allows, you could purchase a special sheet set, a special stuffed animal or character as a bedtime buddy, or you could allow your child to choose a special night light for his room. (A note about nightlights: Make sure the nightlight is not too bright, or it will interfere with the melatonin in your child's system. Melatonin is the sleep hormone). Some parents have renovated and decorated the child's room, allowing the child to help in this task, as part of the preparation process.

Remind your child of the checklist that is now ready for her to add check marks or stickers. Prepare yourself for this coming event by pumping yourself with excitement and with resolve to see this through. Decide that bedtime will be an important ritual for you and your child, and that nothing is going to get in the way. Visualize your family a month down the road when you only spend about 20 or 30 minutes of quality time getting your child to bed, and afterward having an hour or two to spend on yourself or to spend with your spouse before retiring for the night.

The Fourth Step

Begin!

A Typical Bedtime Scenario from the Beginning

Let's go through a typical bedtime scenario of parents who want to make some positive changes in how their child is going to bed. Your child has been staying up until about eleven o'clock, which is the time that you would normally go to bed, and you have been taking your child to bed with you because the child insists. You have chosen a Friday night to begin, and you have made all the preparations. The special sheets are on your child's bed, the special stuffed animal waits in the bedroom, and the night-light is burning. You have already discussed with your child what the bedtime routine will look like, and you have a chart ready for check marks.

You have allowed an hour to get through this new routine on the first night. For this first week or two, you plan to try to get your child to sleep by ten-thirty. Then you will slowly move bedtime up to where eventually your child is going to bed at eight o'clock.

For this first night, however, with a ten-thirty target, you let your child know at 9:00 that in thirty minutes she will need to begin getting ready for bed. This allows her time to wind down and to "finish" what she is doing. Since her play is her work, she needs time to work through her present "problem" in her play. You let her know again at 9:15, that there are 15 more minutes of playtime, and you issue another alert at 9:25 that only five minutes remain.

At nine-thirty, you begin. Depending on your child, the night, the child's day, this could go well or it could be a struggle. Let's not kid ourselves. You have a strong-willed child. This is going to be a struggle. You maintain your firmness and your resolve. You do not yell or get angry. Firmness is the key. You remember to not argue with your child, and instead go straight to your bottom line, which is, "It is time to get ready for bed." You show her the chart of what needs to be checked off. She may not be as impressed as she had been earlier. You maintain your enthusiasm about the chart, and you make the checkmarks if she refuses.

74 | CREATING CALM FROM CHAOS

She may decide after you make the first mark that she does want to make the other check marks, or she may not. You may need to make all the checkmarks in the beginning. Eventually, she will decide that she wants to do this task.

Let's say Item #1 on the checklist is "Put on Pajamas." You take her to the bedroom, pull out two sets of pajamas, and ask her which set she wants to wear tonight. She may dawdle and not make a choice until you force the issue. Then no matter which set you chose, she wants the other one. Go with her choice tonight. There are many battles you must win yet tonight. This doesn't need to be one of them. Anyway, pajamas get put on, with or without your help, depending on your child's abilities and her wishes. Then a checkmark is made and the next item is read.

Let's say Item #2 on the checklist is "Brush Teeth." You help expedite this activity as much as possible. When the teeth are brushed, the checkmark is made on the chart.

Item #3 (or at some point on the chart) says, "Go to the Potty," and Item #4 says, "Get a Drink." It is important to add these to your checklist so that the child does not use these as a reason to get out of bed later. They flow well with brushing teeth since that is also a bathroom activity.

Let's say Item #5 is "Listen to a Story." You and your child go to the bookcase, and your child chooses the book for you to read. If you have more than one child, each child gets to choose a book. Story time aids in helping your child to unwind and get drowsy. You don't want this time to be short-changed. Make it fun. Use a variety of voices for the different characters in the story. Ask questions along the way to keep your child engaged. Enjoy yourself and have fun reading the story. If, on this first night, your child refuses to choose a story, you can make the choice. He will become more cooperative as the week wears on and he sees how fun it is to read with you.

You can sit on the edge or you can lie down on your child's bed to read the story. If you lie down, she is under the covers, but you stay out. It is important that you don't get under the covers with your child, which could give the false hope to your

BEDTIME | 75

child that you are going to sleep with her. Another possible position is that you can sit in the middle of the bed with your child in your lap. The main point is that you have the child ON the bed. If you sit in a rocking chair in the room to read the story, getting your child over to the bed can be a battle. When you are finished with the story, a check mark is made on the chart.

Item #6 may be "Say Prayers." You and your child may kneel beside the bed or you may say them while the child is in bed, whichever stance you choose. I usually say the prayer, a line at a time, and the child repeats. After a while, the child is saying the prayer with me, and then finally I can say, "Let me hear your prayers," and the child says them on her own. We use this common childhood prayer:

> Now I lay me
> down to sleep.
> I pray the Lord
> my soul to keep.
> May angels watch me
> through the night
> and wake me with
> the morning light.
> God bless Mommy,
> and Daddy, etc.
> Amen.

Once a checkmark is made on the chart for the prayers, the next item may be "Tuck In." You tuck her in, give her a kiss, and that is done. The last item on the chart may be "Turn Off Light." Have your child to make the checkmark first, so you can lay aside the chart. Then you tell your child you will be right outside her door, but you will not talk to her again until morning. Then turn off the light, and say your nightly closer, such as "Sweet dreams," or "Good night, my darling," or whatever you choose. Sit in a chair or on the floor outside your child's door.

76 | CREATING CALM FROM CHAOS

Eventually you will be able to go on with your own nightly routine. However, for now you will be busy keeping your child in bed. Whenever your child comes to the door, which she will, you avoid talking to her. If you talk to her, you are giving positive reinforcement for her getting out of bed. You lead her back to bed, retuck her into the bed, and go back to your station outside her door.

You are staying right outside her door at this point so that you can catch her before she leaves her room. Also, she feels comforted when you are close, and this is a good transition from having you right next to her on the bed.

Count the number of times that you have to retuck her into bed, because you will see this number decrease, and you need the encouragement. Sometimes, you will tuck her in, and she practically beats you to the door. You just matter-of-factly return her to her bed. Keep in mind that you only have to put her into bed *one more time* than the number of times that she gets out of bed and you have won! When you win, you both win. When she wins, you both lose.

Eventually, when you continue to calmly return her to her bed, she will come to the conclusion, "This is not working; mom/dad won't let me out of bed," and she will give in to your authority. I promise you: She will give up if you do not give up.

With time, the bedtime routine becomes a comfort to her. Predictability is a great comfort to children. They like to know what is coming. Once this routine begins to take hold, you can use this time to read, work with your laptop, work crossword puzzles, scrapbook, etc. She will be comforted knowing you are close. After about a week of her not leaving her bed, you will be able to start going off to do the nighttime tasks you need to do or to spend some quality time with your mate. With patience and with your consistency, this desired ending will happen.

Once established, it is important to keep the consistency, even on the weekend. Small children do not understand the concept that this is the weekend so we don't have to go by the usual rules. While she is small, her bedtime must be a consideration in all of your weekend plans. When she gets older, perhaps six or eight, depending on your child, she will be able to understand that she gets to stay up a little later on the weekends, if that fits better into your family's plans. She must not return to your bed, however.

Yet there is one exception to your child coming to your bed. If she comes on rare occasions in the middle of the night, because she has had a bad dream, there is no place that feels safer to her than in your bed. However, as soon as she goes back to sleep, return her to her own bed. She needs to wake up in her own bed.

When I was a little girl and had a bad dream, I could go to my parents' room. My mother would lift the cover, and I would slide into bed beside her. She would put her arms around me, and I felt safe. If I was too scared to leave my bed, my parents would hear me crying and my father would come in and lie down beside me. Both of these were sources of great comfort to me when I was a little girl with a big imagination and a bad nightmare.

CHAPTER TWELVE:
WHAT CHILDREN SHOULD NOT HAVE THIS FORM OF DISCIPLINE

There is only a small percentage of children who should not have the Effective Time-Out method of discipline used. If the child has been sexually abused, caution should be used. I would not recommend holding down a child who had been held down and raped. A certain amount of healing within the child needs to take place before this discipline could be administered.

When they are further in their healing, a restraint could serve as comfort and as a demonstration that holding can be positive. However, if holding the child brings on sexually acting-out behaviors, the holding will need to be stopped and replaced with other discipline methods. Whether or not to use this form of discipline depends on the level of healing that has taken place within the child. A professional, whether the pediatrician or the child's counselor, can help a parent or foster parent to make this determination.

Other children who may need special consideration before choosing ETO are those who have been diagnosed with Pervasive Developmental Disorders, which falls into the autism spectrum. Sometimes these youngsters have issues with being touched. Even hugs are difficult for them. Again, holding them for the restraint could prove to be too uncomfortable for them. A parent's discretion is necessary to decide if this method of discipline is even to be considered. Then a consult with a professional may be in order.

There may be other children who would not benefit from the Effective Time-out. Each case needs to be decided on its own merit. This method was developed for normal, healthy, strong-willed children, and they will greatly benefit, as will the entire family of these children, when the Effective Time-Out helps the strong-willed child to learn self-control and obedience to his authority figures. I have seen it work miracles. I hope you find it to be the Godsend for which you have been looking.

Happy parenting!

CHAPTER THIRTEEN:
TESTIMONIALS

I asked some of the parents who have used Effective Time-Out to answer a few questions concerning their experiences with it. These are people who have been using ETO from as little as 2 months to as long as 4 years. What follows are my questions and their responses.

How has ETO worked for your child?

Before I began using ETO, time-outs didn't work. ETO has made a big difference.

ETO works extremely well.

ETO provides guidelines for reinforcement without the use of corporal punishment. It provides the child a positive way to manage and control their behavior.

It works!

ETO is effective.

ETO taught my child how to do time-outs, and eventually taught him to eliminate bad behaviors.

Children know what to expect with ETO.

ETO has been very effective in teaching self-regulation, limit setting, and consequences.

What was the hardest part of using ETO?

Staying with it when you have a strong-willed child.

Consistency.

Being consistent.

Just getting into the routine of using ETO.

Having patience on my end.

What were your thoughts when the technique was first presented to you? Have your thoughts changed? If so, how?

When I first heard of ETO, I didn't think it would really make a difference, but it really makes time-out a punishment that children don't want, whereas before children would prefer time-out over something else.

I wasn't sure it would help, but since using ETO, I've found that it works great.

My initial thought was relief that I had some positive and effective guidelines to follow in disciplining my child. Now I realize what a challenge it can be, and can say, it's definitely worth the challenge.

I did not know how it could be effective. Now there's been a big change and her behaviors have changed.

I felt good about it and hoped it would help—I now KNOW it works!

As a fellow therapist, I could not wait to try to see how it works in two weeks. It did!! It is great to see happy parents.

Have you, or would you recommend the use of ETO to other parents who are struggling with a strong-willed child?

Yes, I think it has been very effective with strong-willed children.

Yes, yes, yes!

I recommend it all the time.

Absolutely.

I have often recommended ETO to other parents. I have even presented some examples, especially since I use ETO in all areas of my child's life. So, for example, our family friends visit our house, I will do an ETO, and they realize how effective it really is.

Yes, I really believe it helps define the role of the parent and the child. It is a good way to discipline strong-willed children.

ETO has helped our family.

Made in the USA
Charleston, SC
25 November 2011